Festivals and Celebrations

By Caryn Jenner

US Senior Editor Shannon Beatty
Editors Kritika Gupta, Olivia Stanford
Art Editors Radhika Banerjee, Emma Hobson, Kanika Kalra
Jacket Co-ordinator Francesca Young
Jacket Designers Dheeraj Arora, Amy Keast
DTP Designers Nityanand Kumar, Dheeraj Singh
Picture Researcher Aditya Katyal
Producer, Pre-Production Nadine King
Producer Niamh Tierney
Managing Editors Monica Saigal, Laura Gilbert
Managing Art Editors Neha Ahuja Chowdhry, Diane Peyton Jones
Art Director Martin Wilson
Publisher Sarah Larter
Publishing Director Sophie Mitchell

Reading Consultant Linda Gambrell, Ph.D.
Subject Consultants Dr. Alasdair Richardson, Rhiannon Love

First American Edition, 2017
Published in the United States by DK Publishing
345 Hudson Street, New York, New York 10014

A catalog record for this book is available from the Library of Congress.
ISBN: 978-1-4654-6318-0 (Paperback)
ISBN: 978-1-4654-6319-7 (Hardcover)

DK books are available at special discounts when purchased in bulk for sales promotions,
premiums, fund-raising, or educational use. For details, contact:
DK Publishing Special Markets,
345 Hudson Street, New York, New York 10014
SpecialSales@dk.com

Printed and bound in China.

The publisher would like to thank the following for their kind permission to reproduce their photographs:
(Key: a-above; b-below/bottom; c-center; f-far; l-left; r-right; t-top)
1 123RF.com: (Colours). **4 Getty Images**: Pacific Press / LightRocket (b). **5 Dreamstime.com**: Anand Kanthan (c). **iStockphoto.
com**: ross1248 (bc). **6–7 Alamy Stock Photo**: Dinendra Haria (b). **7 Dorling Kindersley**: Barnabas Kindersley (cr). **8 Getty
Images**: Pacific Press (cb); Craig Pershouse (ca). **9 Dreamstime.com**: Kikujungboy (t); Mmeeds (cb). **10–11 Alamy Stock Photo**:
Anil Kumar. **12 123RF.com**: Noam Armonn (bl). **14–15 123RF.com**: Jennifer Barrow (b). **15 Alamy Stock Photo**: imageBROKER
(t). **16–17 123RF.com**: nui7711. **18–19 Dreamstime.com**: Pablo Hidalgo. **20–21 Dreamstime.com**: Ig0rzh. **22–23 Dreamstime.
com**: Picturetheworld (t). **24 iStockphoto.com**: lovleah (c); mmeee (bc). **25 123RF.com**: Valentyna Chukhlyebova (b).
Dreamstime.com: Vdvtut (t). **28–29 Getty Images**: Sollina Images. **29 123RF.com**: Fernando Gregory Milan (crb). **30–31 Alamy
Stock Photo**: Indiapicture (b). **33 123RF.com**: Eugene Bochkarev. **34 Dreamstime.com**: Goldenkb (crb). **35 Dreamstime.com**:
Noam Armonn. **36 Getty Images**: Brand X Pictures (c). **38–39 Getty Images**: Mark Adams. **40–41 Dreamstime.com**: Serrnovik

Jacket images: *Front*: **Alamy Stock Photo**: Sabena Jane Blackbird cb, Dinendra Haria crb;
Depositphotos Inc: alphaspirit (Background); **Getty Images**: Pan Hong tc
Endpaper images: *Front*: **123RF.com**: Liana Manukyan; *Back*: **123RF.com**: Liana Manukyan

All other images © Dorling Kindersley
For further information see: www.dkimages.com

A WORLD OF IDEAS:
SEE ALL THERE IS TO KNOW

www.dk.com

Contents

Chapter 1
Happy New Year!

It is New Year's Eve. The New Year begins at midnight. Colorful fireworks are set off.

New York, USA

People have parties with friends and family. They celebrate the start of the New Year.

London, United Kingdom

Sydney, Australia

5

Chinese New Year is in January or February. Dancers parade a colorful dragon through the streets. The dragon is meant to scare away evil spirits. It also brings good luck.

People performing a dragon dance.

Red is said to be a lucky color.
Children receive red envelopes
with money inside!

Red envelopes

More world festivals

Here are some more festivals. They are celebrated throughout the year.

The New Yam Festival celebrates the autumn harvest in West Africa. Yams are eaten and there is dancing.

Sikh New Year is celebrated in April across the world. There is music and dancing. It is also called Vaisakhi.

Buddha Day celebrates the life of the Buddha. In spring in Chiang Mai, Thailand, candles are lit.

Huge parades are held during spring for Carnival. One of the biggest is in Rio de Janeiro, Brazil.

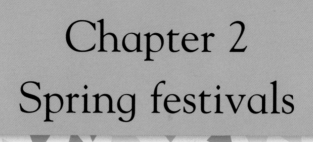

Chapter 2
Spring festivals

Holi is the Hindu festival of color. It celebrates good over evil. Holi happens in February or March.

People start celebrating the night before. They sing and dance. The next day they throw special powder paint at each other. They also throw colored water. It is a lot of fun and very messy!

The bright colors celebrate the start of spring.

11

Passover lasts for a week. It is in March or April. During Passover, Jewish families gather for a special meal. This is called the "Seder." Together, they read the story of Moses.

People eat special foods during Passover. One is a flat cracker called "matzo."

Each food on the Seder plate
has a special meaning.

A long time ago, Moses led
the Jews to freedom. Passover
celebrates their freedom.

Easter is a spring festival. It happens between March and May. Christians believe Jesus was the Son of God. He was killed by the Romans. Christians believe that after three days he came back to life. Easter remembers this.

Easter celebrates new life. People dye eggs in bright spring colors.

People go to church at Easter
to remember Jesus' return to life.

15

People at the Cherry Blossom
Festival in Osaka, Japan.

16

In Japan, cherry blossoms are very special flowers. They grow on cherry trees for a short time every spring. People gather to look at the flowers during the Cherry Blossom Festival. They have picnics under the trees with family and friends. This festival is also known as hanami.

Chapter 3
Summer festivals

Midsummer's Day is the day of the year with the most sunlight.

A Midsummer's Day celebration in Sweden.

Many people celebrate with parties and parades. Some people gather to watch the sunrise. In Sweden, people dance around a midsummer pole.

Ramadan is a holy month for Muslims. They do not eat or drink between sunrise and sunset. This is to bring them closer to God. It also reminds them of the suffering of the poor.

Muslims celebrate the end of Ramadan with a festival called Eid al-Fitr. People enjoy feasts and give gifts on Eid.

A crescent moon marks the start of Ramadan. This is the Blue Mosque in Istanbul, Turkey.

The 4th of July is Independence Day. It marks the day when the United States became a new country.

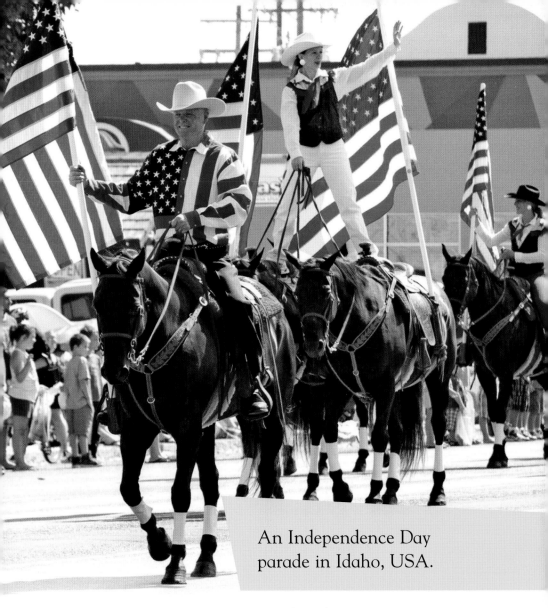

An Independence Day parade in Idaho, USA.

Americans wear clothes in red, white, and blue. They also wave American flags. There are parades, picnics, and fireworks.

National days

Many countries have their own national day. They celebrate a country's history and culture.

Australia Day celebrates Australian history and culture.

French flags are put up for the French National Day. It is also called Bastille day.

On Canada Day there are parades in the street.

German Unity Day celebrates Germany being rejoined as one country.

Chapter 4
Fall festivals

Halloween is on October 31st. It is also known as All Hallows' Eve.

People used to think that evil spirits came out. They dressed in frightening costumes to protect themselves. Now, children dress up in costumes. They also make pumpkins into jack-o'-lanterns.

Jack-o'-lantern

Children dress up in costumes to celebrate Halloween.

A girl wears face
paint for the Day of
the Dead celebration.

The Mexican Day of the Dead sounds like a sad holiday. In fact, it is very lively! Parties and parades are held to remember people who have died.

People decorate the graves of loved ones with flowers and candles.

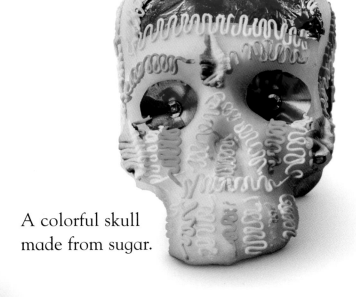

A colorful skull made from sugar.

Diwali is the Hindu festival of lights. It celebrates good over evil. People light special clay lamps, called "diyas."

People celebrate with feasts
and fireworks. They also pray to
Lakshmi, the goddess of wealth.

Families make colorful "rangoli"
patterns for Diwali.

On Thanksgiving, Americans gather for a special family feast.

In 1620, people from Europe arrived in America. They nearly ran out of food in the new land. Native Americans helped them plant new crops. The Europeans invited the Native Americans to a harvest feast. This was the first Thanksgiving.

Pumpkin pie is a popular dessert during Thanksgiving.

Turkey is usually served as part of a Thanksgiving dinner.

Chapter 5
Winter festivals

Hanukkah is a Jewish celebration that is usually in December. Many years ago, the Jews had to rebuild their temple. They had enough oil to light their lamps for only one day. Amazingly, the lamps stayed lit for eight days.

Jews light candles on a menorah to remember this.

People play a game with a spinning top called a "dreidel."

Hanukkah lasts for eight days. Each night, people light one more candle on the menorah until all eight are lit.

At Christmas, Christians celebrate the birth of Jesus. People decorate Christmas trees and give each other presents.

Many years ago, Saint Nicholas gave his money to help poor people. Some people called him Santa Claus, or Father Christmas.

Now, children hope Santa will bring them Christmas presents.

Children act out Jesus' birth in nativity plays.

The festival of Kwanzaa celebrates African family and culture.

Kwanzaa lasts for a week. Each night, families light special candles. They enjoy feasts, music, and dancing!

A family lighting special Kwanzaa candles.

Children's Day

Hurray for Children's Day!
It's a special day for children
around the world.

Children everywhere need safe homes and healthy food. They also need to play and to learn. Children's Day remembers the importance of these things.

Quiz

 1. Dragon parades are part of which festival?

 2. On which festival do people throw colored water at each other?

 3. During which festival do people eat "matzo"?

 4. Name the West African autumn harvest festival.

 5. Which celebration takes place on the day with the most sunlight?

6 What do Americans celebrate on the 4th of July?

 7 What is another name for the Cherry Blossom Festival?

 8 Which festival is celebrated at the end of Ramadan?

 9 On which festival do people decorate the graves of their loved ones?

 10 On which festival do people dye eggs?

Answers on page 45

Glossary

culture
includes the language, art, music, clothes, food, and beliefs of a group of people

feast
special meal with lots of food

grave
place in the ground where a dead person is buried

harvest
activity of cutting and collecting crops from the fields

holy
related to God, gods, or religion

menorah
special object that can hold up to nine candles

national
to do with a certain country

nativity
birth of Jesus Christ

parade
group of people walking from one place to another, often in costume

rangoli
art of using colored sand or powder to create patterns on the floor

spirit
ghostly being

suffering
pain caused by injury, illness, or loss

wealth
having a lot of something, especially money

yam
type of vegetable

Answers to the quiz:

1. Chinese New Year; 2. Holi; 3. Passover;
4. The New Yam Festival; 5. Midsummer's Day;
6. Independence Day; 7. Hanami; 8. Eid al-Fitr;
9. The Day of the Dead; 10. Easter

Guide for Parents

This book is part of an exciting four-level reading series for children, developing the habit of reading widely for both pleasure and information. These chapter books have a compelling main narrative to suit your child's reading ability. Each book is designed to develop your child's reading skills, fluency, grammar awareness, and comprehension in order to build confidence and engagement when reading.

Ready for a *Level 2* book

YOUR CHILD SHOULD

- be familiar with using beginning letter sounds and context clues to figure out unfamiliar words.
- be aware of the need for a slight pause at commas and a longer one at periods.
- alter his/her expression for questions and exclamations.

A VALUABLE AND SHARED READING EXPERIENCE

For many children, reading requires much effort, but adult participation can make this both fun and easier. So here are a few tips on how to use this book with your child.

TIP 1 Check out the contents together before your child begins:

- read the text about the book on the back cover.
- flip through the book and stop to chat about the contents page together to heighten your child's interest and expectation.
- make use of unfamiliar or difficult words on the page in a brief discussion.
- chat about the nonfiction reading features used in the book, such as headings, captions, or labels.

TIP 2 Support your child as he/she reads the story pages:

- give the book to your child to read and turn the pages.

- where necessary, encourage your child to break a word into syllables, sound out each one, and then flow the syllables together. Ask him/her to reread the sentence to check the meaning.

- you may need to help read some new vocabulary words that are difficult for your child to sound out.

- when there's a question mark or an exclamation point, encourage your child to vary his/her voice as he/she reads the sentence. Demonstrate how to do this if it is helpful.

TIP 3 Chat at the end of each page:

- ask questions about the text and the meaning of the words used. These help to develop comprehension skills and awareness of the language used.

A FEW ADDITIONAL TIPS

- Always encourage your child to try reading difficult words by themselves. Praise any self-corrections, for example, "I like the way you sounded out that word and then changed the way you said it, to make sense."

- Try to read together everyday. Reading little and often is best. These books are divided into manageable chapters for one reading session. However, after 10 minutes, only keep going if your child wants to read on.

- Read other books of different types to your child just for enjoyment and information.

Series consultant, **Dr. Linda Gambrell**, Distinguished Professor of Education at Clemson University, has served as President of the National Reading Conference, the College Reading Association, and the International Reading Association.

Index